A Mind of Many Mirrors

To the voices in my head, thanks for keeping me company and inspiring some truly bizarre poetry.

And, to the thesaurus, for making me sound smarter than I really am.

Introduction

 We are all made of fragments, pieces of truth scattered across shifting perspectives. Each of us is a patchwork of moments, experiences, and emotions, reflected in the mirrors of our lives, each one showing a different angle, a different version of who we are. A Mind of Many Mirrors is an attempt to gather those reflections, to look at the complexities of love, loss, and the spaces in between.

In these pages, you'll find poems about the timeless ache of love and the complexity of desire, the kind of romance that feels like it was written in another century, but still beats in the chest of today. But just as easily, you'll be pulled into the darker corners of human experience—heartbreak, the suffocating grip of forced decisions, and the fragile, messy art of letting go.

This collection isn't just personal. It's about the world too, the ones we live in and the ones we inherit. t's about grief, social media's subtle cruelty, the weight of corporate culture, and the haunting influence of capitalism. It's about history, about remembering and confronting the past.

It's about the stories we tell ourselves to survive, and the ones we're told to forget. I don't expect these poems to change your life or provide all the answers. I just hope they resonate with something inside you, like a mirror that doesn't just reflect your face but something deeper, something hidden. Maybe it will make you pause, or think, or see something in a new way.

Passion

Beauty

She is like the first dew on a tender leaf,

A softness that touches the soul—delicate,

Yet stronger than you can ever imagine.

Her beauty is a wild bloom that thrives in silence,

A flower with petals woven from the dawn's first light,

She opens her heart to the world in secret,

Spreading a fragrance that never asks for praise.

Her face is the moonlit sea, quiet and eternal,

A pearl, soft and glowing,

found in the depths of the earth,

Rich in mystery, in quiet power,

Untouched by time, a symbol of all that is pure.

She is both the stillness of a moment

and the knowledge it brings,

Beauty and intellect bound together,

like the moon and the tide.

Serene

She's like a warmth of sunrays on a winter morning,

A gentle touch of hope, without a word, a warning.

Through frosted panes, her smile does gently gleam,

A fleeting glimpse of solace in a world of frozen dream.

Stay By My Side

Ask me if I'm okay.

When I say I'm fine, Ask me again.

Because I'm not.

I am breaking inside.

I want you to be the anchor of my sanity,

Stay by my side.

I know it's getting late and you should go,

But I want you to stay,

I know you love me,

But I want to hear you say.

I need you to grasp me, hold me tightly.

Talking what we already know,

Just don't go.

Everything now seems useless,

Everyone is so cold, so ruthless.

But your vibe is unmatchable,

Nobody I repeat nobody can make me feel the same comfort as you,

No, I'm not saying it just to make you stay by side, believe me, honestly, it's true.

I need your support,

I just need to feel your presence,

I need your touch.

Am I asking for too much?

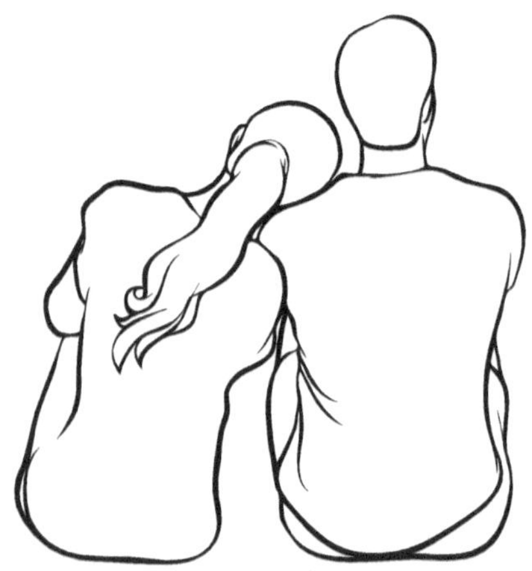

Real Intimacy

It is not grand like the sunsets she love,
Thousands of colors spilled across the sky,
It is in little things,
Like our hands brushing against each other,
Before holding mine, firmly,
giving our hearts an instant high.

It's the smell of your hair when you lie on my chest,
the intimacy of her silence,
simply cannot be expressed.

It's the conversations,
the fun ones with giggles and tickles,
the serious and focused ones,
or simply sitting silent,
in each other's arms,
at the lake,
legs swinging in water,
watching the ripples.

She resting her head on my back,
hugging me from behind,
as we ride through the busy streets.

She letting me play with her beloved hair,
Asking me to braid them,
And donning my bad work for rest of the day.

It's sharing deepest desires and darkest fears,
and the truly compassionate listening,
It's understanding beyond mere words,
that closeness is beyond sexual touch
— Spiritually resonating.

Just You & Me

I want to be yours,
But I wonder,
Do you want me too?
Maybe you do.
Maybe you love me more,
In the silence of "just us two,"
When the world fades away,
And it's only me and you.

You transform— like the quiet sea breaking into
waves.
You cast off the armor of silence,
letting your spirit roam free.
I see the wilderness in your eyes,
I wonder if you know how beautiful you are in those
moments—
unapologetically free, fearlessly you.

I dream of a little cabin,
hidden where the world cannot find us.
Just you, just me, and the infinite possibilities of us.

Take me with you

Take me to the library,
Let us watch the words smile.
that conveys what our hearts carry,
watching the sad phase beguile.

Take me to the art gallery,
hold my hand in the longer line,
wait and judge if art is satisfactory,
while I'll admire what's mine.

Yes, She's Different

Yes, she is different
She's a poisonous antidote to all toxicity,
Alas, she doesn't know she carries a spark,
Capable of burning life's infelicity.
She's the definition of perfect, a little exaggerated?
But I can say because I have observed;
intrigued and been completely fascinated.

In a world full of fake people,
She's also genuine, no seduction, no deception
A warm understanding,
With no confusion,
She is always new yet pure,
Blessing us with her care.

She's different
From heart where only the truth resided,
where honesty finally lived
No intentions to outwit, play games or cause pain,
Putting all her efforts,
shame it went waste without gain.

Love Story

Separated while our love was in its incipience,

She became Penelope to my Odysseus,

Even in the face of an uncertain future, I'm certain

about loyalty on her end,

Why she loves me so much I simply can't comprehend.

Waris said God created love,

It was God Himself that first loved,

But society has placed casteism higher above,

She became Heer to my Ranjh as our story roved.

My Queen is like CLEOPATRA,

Our story will be MARKed legendary, will be told and

retold like Panchatantra,

She could have anything, anyone she wants,

Many become envious when she choose me & flaunts.

Our love, a story of resilience,

Two hearts that refused to yield in the face of any

hindrance,

Amidst life's challenges, our bond remains a constant,

For in her love, I find my solace, my heart, forever

content.

Carving Out Forever

In the dusk of uncertain days,

where shadows stretch long and heavy,

we found ourselves wandering,

not lost but seeking,

two souls adrift in the murmur of the world.

The secret meetings,

in whispered corners where the night

held its breath,

we built a world of hushed tones

and stolen glances,

a world fragile,

like the first light of dawn

that trembles on the edge of night.

There were the voices,

a chorus of doubt,

echoing in the corridors of our minds,

yet we pressed on,

weighed down but not broken,

our love a thing of endurance,

not of flight.

In the mirror of our parents' eyes,
we saw the reflection of our hopes,
clear yet distant,
and we filled the space between with dreams,
we painted over the cracks with a brush dipped in faith,
and in time, they too began to see.

And now, as the world spins on,
we find ourselves beneath the warmth of a foreign sun,
soaring through the skies for the first time,
over sparkling beaches and emerald islands,
where sea caves whisper secrets to the waves.
On the sands of Phuket,
where the ocean breathes softly against the shore,
and time seems to forget its place.

A month has passed,
and in that brief eternity,
we have carved out a piece of forever,
not just as lovers,
but as friends,
as two who have weathered the storm,
who have seen the darkness and chosen the light.

Stillness In Turmoil

While everything around me whirls and storms,

I remain grounded.

In the middle of all the turmoil

of all the intense energies and emotions,

When it's all just so dark,

I cannot see anything,

cannot touch or hear.

I think about you,

My heart feels your love.

And I get clarity.

With no pause between my thoughts,

Our love transforms into motivational poetry.

There is a stillness.

In your love.

To find this pure, true love,

I'll remain grounded in thousands of worldly storms to come.

To find you on the other side.

Pleasure

Raw & Pure

As I lean her back
against the wall
I lift her skirt
and feel her body call
Her curves and her skin
I crave every inch
Her dark eyes pierce mine
As my heart begins to flinch

She whispers to me,
"Take me, my love"
And in that moment
I know there's nothing above
No words are needed,
As I explore her flesh
My fingers leave marks
And claim her as my own, afresh

My heart pounds and gasps
As she trembles in my arms
Her ink spills out
All over me, with no qualms
The heat rushes through us
As we satisfy our cravings

In this moment of passion
We're no longer just mere beings

For now, in this moment
All we have is each other
Our love is raw and pure
As we lose ourselves in the pleasure.

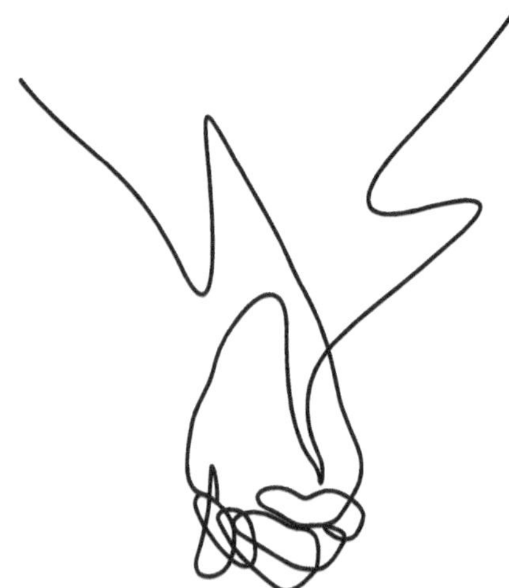

Passionate Act

The night draped us in a blanket of desire,
Passion that burned like an unquenchable fire,
Your limbs entangled mine, like vines in the wild,
drawing us closer, as we listened to songs you
compiled.

Your grip on my hips was fierce and true,
A primal hunger that I felt anew,
My face nestled in your bosom, soft and warm,
A sense of safety that could weather any storm.

Our bodies fused together like wax,
Melted and sculpted in the heat of passionate acts.

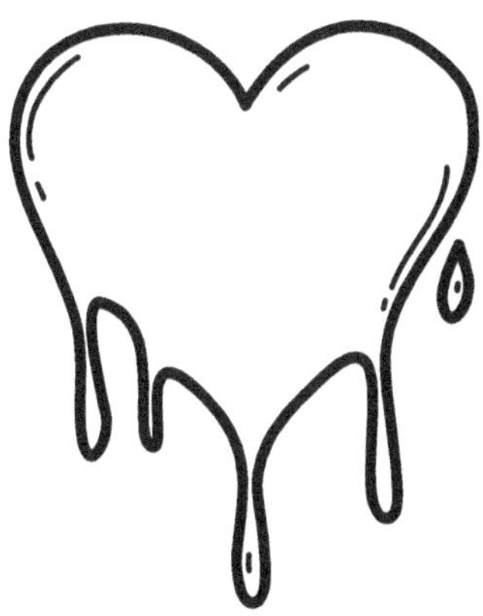

Blessing

Oh starry night, how you gaze upon us,
Your magic blesses me, as I behold,
My love, flaunting her cute smile,
Hiding her wildness, behind traditional attire,
Knowing what we share is beyond words, I'm afraid,
Will my words do justice to what I feel?
It is not just passion,
Nor the simple vanity of our hearts,
It is a divine fire within.

Oh Yes

The flicker of your lips in my mind's eye,
Sets my body on a familiar high
The thought of our tongues intertwining
Overwhelms me with sensations, so enticing

Your eyes meet mine, my heart races fast
I want you to keep looking, make this moment last
Let your gaze pierce into my very soul
Consuming me with love, making me whole

With each passing moment, the heat within me grows
A lustful fire building, from my head to toes
I want to be consumed by this passion tonight
Revel in it until our bodies ache with delight

My fingers twitch with desire,
and I can't help but imagine slipping them inside your
quagmire,
feeling your wetness as you moan with pleasure.
I want to be lost in the moment, consumed by the raw
intensity of our hunger.

I want to feel your creamy love as it spills out of your
sensitive zone,
mingling with the sweetest cream of my own.
I want to be consumed by the sensation of our bodies
moving together and sway
in the primal pleasure of physical play.

I yearn to merge with you,
feel being one and true.
Consumed by passion, our bodies intertwined maze,
Together we burn, in love and lust's fiery daze.

And as we come together,
I want our eyes to lock once more,
Our love spilling out of us in a creamy mess
And your orgasmic moaning of "oh yes".

Unleashed

My emotions run wild, unleashed by drink,
My desires take over, I cannot think.
Running after my lust, down the street I chase,
In you, I see my paradise, my secret place.

I long to share with you my deepest longing,
My sexual interests, my fetishes so strong.
My mind races from the crown of your head,
To the soles of your feet, my hunger widespread.

Your hair graces the back of your neck so fine,
Golden brown with black streaks, so divine.
Let down, your kinkiness hidden beneath your guise,
Seductive and mature, a feast for my eyes.

Your exotic aroma tempts me to caress,
Making me want to taste you, nothing less.
I run my tongue along the smoothness of your nape,
Excitement building with every taste of your shape.

Devouring every inch, I kiss your shoulder,
Leaving my mark, I know I'll come back bolder.
Moving to your chest, a vast beauty to behold,
Kissing between the valley, your breasts so bold .

On my bed, I lay you down, so pure,
Grabbing your nipples, squeezing them for sure.
Harder and harder, your sweet moaning voice,
Pleasuring myself, a great rejoice.

My tongue roaming reaches below your waist,
Tasting your essence, it is the best.
Your taste is so poisonous, it fills me whole,
Moving from left to right, I devour your soul.

Will you give me more, I ask with a sigh,
As my lips are stained with your poison, I cannot deny.

Afterglow

Delicate and gentle, her touch did explore,
Riding the storm out, we came to the shore.
Flushed with love, we collapsed in content,
A midnight testament, to the passion we had spent.

Her joy was palpable, despite the pleasure and pain,
Like a flower in bloom after the rain.
Bruised and beautiful, a work of art in motion,
Resting there, elated, in a love-fueled emotion.

Grateful and smiling, she thanked me for the night,
I whispered in her ear, "It was my delight".
Our kisses, mingled with the afterglow,
Soft music played on, its melody slow.

Wrapped up in her embrace, I'm in a state of bliss,
Your cuddles are my escape from the chaos.
Discussing new ways we want to explore,
Ways to quell insecurities and adore.

Happiness in the moment, beyond measure,
As she lays her head on my chest, I treasure.
Never thought, I'd find someone so close,
Completing me, making me whole, she arose.

Sex In Cemetery

The ghostly audience cheered
For a feeling that they will never taste again,
As we breathed life into a place all about death,
Experiencing pleasure and pain.

Amidst the tombstones grey and still,
We found a love that death could not kill.
In this moment, nothing else mattered, but the
sensation we share,
A primal need that can't be denied, an intoxicating
affair.

The rustling leaves and the creaking trees,
The only sounds in that land of unease,
But in each other's arms, we found a home,
In a place where most would fear to roam.

Our bodies united, a dance of lust and desire,
Each touch sending shivers down my spine,
igniting a fire,
A symphony of moans and whispers,
as we surrendered to the night,
Lost in a world of ecstasy,
where wrong and right lose sight.

Parting

Misunderstood

Misunderstood by love, my heart aches with pain,

For the one I cherish sees me as a stain.

A villain in their eyes, though I've done no wrong,

My love for them unconditional, steadfast and strong.

I've always wished the best, with all that I am,

But still I'm met with accusations and disdain.

My intentions pure, my love for them so real,

But still they cannot see what I truly feel.

I try to make amends, to show them what's true,

But still they see me as a monster through and through.

My heart is breaking, as I stand here all alone,

Misunderstood by love, so far from my home.

But still I hold on, to the hope that they will see,

That my love for them is pure,

and meant to set them free.

And though they may not understand,

I'll love them all the same,

For my love is unconditional, forever unchanging.

Afterthought

Before today, I'd firmly declared,
A vow my heart had always shared:
Love's no arcade, no game to play,
No backup plan, no castaway.
Never an afterthought—I swore,
But now, I question, was I sure?

Standing here, on the edge of this divide,
I feel a pull, impossible to hide.
It's strange, intangible—something unknown,
Rising from depths I thought were my own.

A fire burns, consuming, untamed,
A yearning I can't seem to explain.
Knowing the pain it might ignite,
Yet my heart leads me in one direction tonight.

I'd move mountains, part seas below,
To escape the ache that grips me so.
But the numbness lingers, the grief won't fade,
As I drown in love's unrelenting shade.

It's no easy path—it's sharp, it's steep,

A climb where hearts may soar or weep.

But still, I'll try, I'll dare be bold,

For love is worth it—or so I'm told.

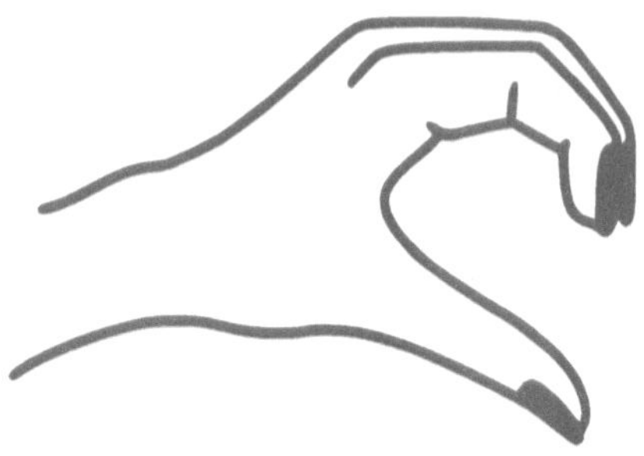

Just Another Dying Rose

Yesterday I felt like I was falling from a ladder,

breaking all the rungs,

only to land on the ground

that would disintegrate beneath me at any moment,

I felt like I'd sink into the earth

and the soft damp soil would fill my lungs.

Thankfully, I am still on solid ground.

I don't think how long I'll survive it,

Even if I,

Will I find the strength to go back

to the place where I was?

Or am I going to be a rose in the garden of your life,

To whom you loved once,

whose fragrance you can still remember,

But once fallen on the ground by flocks of second
thoughts,

I'll be lying on the ground to decay before being
forgotten.

Muse

Though our conversations are few,
My thoughts always drift back to you,
Who do you think I think of when I write of love and
pain,
You know it's you, only you who fills my brain.

For every verse I dare to spin,
Your essence weaves itself within.
Know that it is you who rule my mind,
My muse, my friend, one of a kind.

Our connection may have stretched thin,
But our love is pure and pure within,
So even when we are separated now,
Our love will live, this I vow,
In my every word, in every rhyme,
Your spirit, your soul, will forever chime.

All Is Well?

Amidst the façade of all being well,

A tempest of tears within me dwell.

Though the sky shines with a golden light,

A storm of longing fills my night.

Invisible threads of memories, soft and thin,

Wrap around my soul, tug from within.

Though all seems well in my life,

Missing love cuts like a knife.

Laughter shared and words we said,

Echo in my heart, but now they're dead.

Now I'm haunted by love's sweet ghost,

Its absence, a melancholy host.

A ghost of love, its shadow near,

It haunts me now, it lingers here.

Let tears fall soft, and secrets keep,

In silence where the sorrows sleep.

Though everything seems fine from afar,

Within, I yearn for a guiding star.

Powerlessness

Forced Vows

Once a heart full of love and light,

Now shattered by pain, such a cruel plight,

A mind in turmoil, lost in doubt,

A bride forced to wed, with no way out.

Parents found out, about her love and devotion,

So they took control, made a life changing decision.

What they saw as right, felt wrong inside,

Her heart in agony, for the love she had to hide.

She stands before the sacred flame, in a dress of red,

Her eyes downcast, with tears unshed,

Her mind in chaos, with thoughts undefined,

Of what the future holds, and what she's left behind.

She made a promise, to another's heart,

But now she's married, with a brand new start,

Her dreams of love, now lost in this new reality,

A song of hope now silenced, a tragic fatality.

She wants to speak her truth, to let her love be known,

To break free from these chains, and reclaim what's her own.

But she's a bride, bound by society's decree,

Her voice now silenced, by traditions that won't set her free.

So she takes a breath, and says her vows,

Her heart aching, as she's lost somehow,

But she'll keep her promise, to love and cherish,

And hope that one day, her mind will no longer perish.

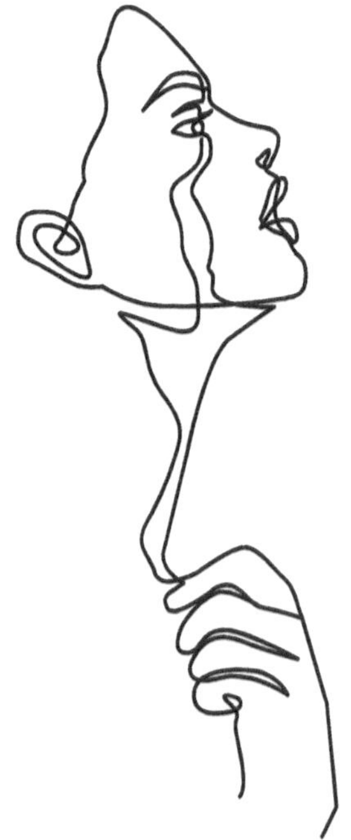

Licence To Rape

Late at night, I lay in fear
Newly married, forced to adhere
Felt like prey in a tiger's lair

He leaned towards me, pretending to seek
Some object placed beside me that he'd need.
But then he pressed his hands upon my lips,
And pinned me down with force and violent grips.

He climbed atop me, spreading wide my thighs,
And gazed into my eyes with hungry, feral eyes.
But as I looked back, I saw through his lies,
And told him no, though he laughed and did not
comply.

He struck me hard, and blood did soon flow,
He satisfied his lust and let his demon show.
The walls around me seemed to sneer and jeer,
As if they knew that I had nowhere to steer.

He inflicted pain, and I endured humiliation,
My soul quivering with fear and trepidation.
Three times he tried and failed to last,
And droplets of my blood upon the sheets were cast.

He reveled in his victory, then fell asleep,
While I lay there, numb and unable to weep.

My clothes and soul, both lay undressed,
Like a monster, he left his marks on my chest.
The once-proud daughter, now filled with shame,
How uncontrollable, my life, my pain.

I wore my sari, my trembling hands,
Fell to the floor, tears, like shattered strands.
Enslaved to a man who took what he pleased,
Leaving me lifeless and forever changed.

Memories

You live like a song stuck in my head,

Echoing words that were never said,

All day, all night, it plays on.

I can't erase, only rewind,

Can't move forward, can't forget,

Just like the memories of you.

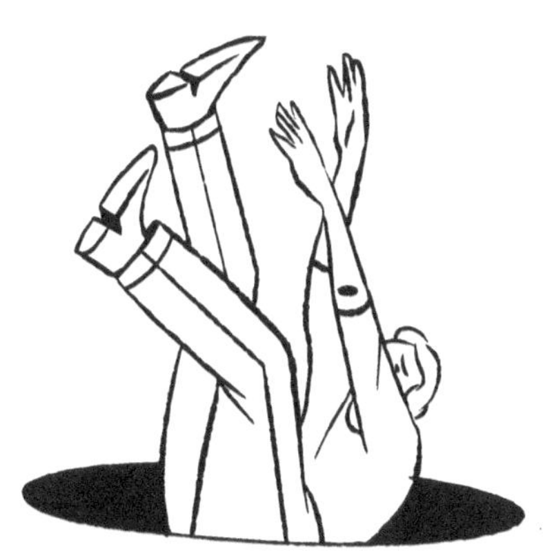

Too Young

Alas, I was too young,

To muster up my courage,

To not let our lovesong left unsung.

Alas I was too young

To find the right words to say

To make it clear,

To make you stay.

Drawn to the Flame

Love,
a fiery inferno in my soul,
burning bright and uncontrolled,
consuming every inch of my being.

She, the object of my desire,
a distant sun, shining so bright,
but her warmth forever out of reach,
leaving me basking in her glow, alone.

I long for her touch, her love,
but all I get in return is cold reality,
my soul aching with the agony of desire.

Like a moth to a flame, I am drawn,
unable to resist her alluring pull,
even as I know it will only bring me pain,
even as I know my heart will be shattered.

But still, I cannot help but yearn,
to be with her, to hold her close,
to feel the warmth of her embrace,
even if it's just for a moment in time.

This love...
a hellish existence I cannot escape,
a constant torment that never abates,
leaving me to suffer in silence, alone.

This Can't Be Our End

I have no concern for the world's chatter,
our love is pure and nothing else will matter,
listen, my dear, to the rhythm of my heart,
it beats for you, and will never fall apart.

I spend my days lost in thought,
Reminiscing about the moments we've caught,
Your memory lingers, haunting my mind,
A love so beautiful, so hard to find.

Your love has taken hold of me,
A feeling so strong, it's all I can see,
I am yours, you are mine, forever bound,
Our love, so beautiful, so profound.

In my dreams, I feel the warmth of your touch,
My heart filled with audacity, it dares to dream and clutch,
Our love is worth every obstacle that we may face,
A love so strong, so beautiful, nothing can replace.

We belong together as our hearts always proclaim,

A love that burns bright, with no shame,

Let us meet, my love, before the end of time,

Our story deserves a better end, for a love that's truly

divine.

Bottled

Amidst the velvety cloak of the ebony night,
As I recline in my solitary solitude,
My senses are awash with memories bright,
of a love that once bloomed, now withered and
subdued.

A bottle of rum, my faithful companion true,
As I sip on its nectar, my thoughts take flight,
Through the mists of time, to moments spent with you,
To a love that was once a shining beacon of light.

In the dimly lit screen, I behold your face,
Etched in pixels, a mere shadow of your grace,
My heart aches for your touch, your embrace.

But time marches on, and you've slipped away,
And yet your memory lingers, like a haunting melody,
A love that was once, now just a forgotten reverie.

And so I write, in words that flow like a river,
Of a love that was, of memories that still quiver,
In the depths of my soul, like a forgotten treasure.

Oh, how I long to be with you again,

To feel the warmth of your touch, to hear your voice,

To bask in the glow of a love that was once so pure,

But alas, fate has other plans, and we must resign,

To a love that once bloomed, but has now declined.

Pivet

Love & Pain

The heart knows no pain in love, they say,

But the brain knows of a different tale.

Though the heart may never feel the pain,

The brain remembers it all.

For the heart can be made whole again,

But the brain will forever fall.

Until both heart and brain unite,

Stop concentrating on the missing piece,

The pain of love shall never cease.

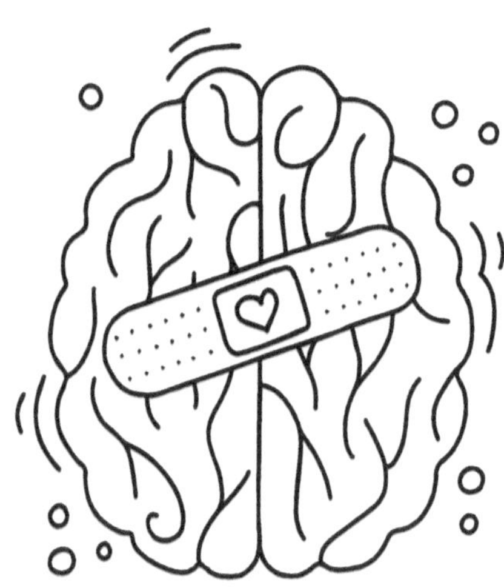

Letting Go

The whispers of our old conversations
Echo softly in my mind
A connection built on true emotions
Now left so far behind

Our paths diverged, as they often do
In this ever-changing life
And though we try to keep in touch
It seems to cause us strife

The loss of someone close to heart
Is a special kind of pain
It's not the anger or the hate
But knowing things won't be the same

We used to talk for hours on end
Sharing secrets, dreams, and fears
But now we barely say a word
And the silence brings me tears

I ache to tell you of my joys
And hear about your days
But the distance now between us
Feels like an endless maze

The silence now between us
Is deafening in its way
I long to bridge the distance
And reconnect in some way

But I have to come to terms with change
It does feel like an endless test
But we must find a way to move on
And find the good in what's left

So here's to what we had, my friend
And to what could have been
I'll hold our memories in my heart
And cherish them within.

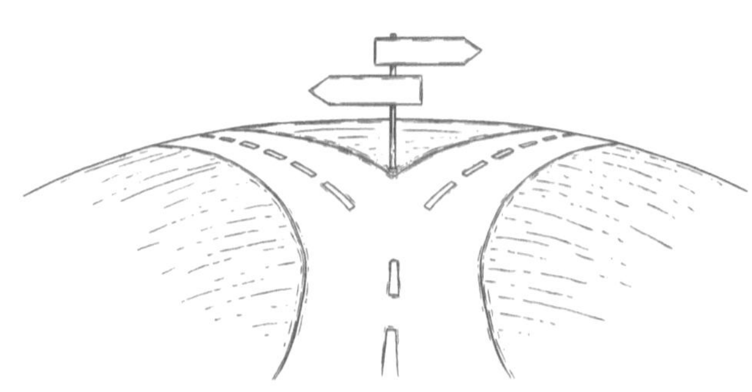

Solace

As the night falls and darkness reigns,
Loneliness grips my heart and drains
All the joy that once was mine,
Leaving me lost in the depths of time.

But even in its dreary presence,
I find a kind of peace,
A moment of stillness,
In this hectic human race.

And then I remember,
Good days, Good people, I've seen a few,
The joy that I have savored,
Then I recall love - I think of you.

And the blissful moments that we've shared,
The emotions we've experienced, so sweet and true,
That brings back the light and chases away the blue.

In your presence, time stands still,
As I relive stories and laughter, until
The night fades and the dawn draws near,
And I'm left with memories so dear.

For though we may be apart,

And distance may strain the heart,

Our love shall always remain,

A flame that no darkness can ever contain.

So as the night fades into day,

And loneliness tries to lead me astray,

I shall hold onto our memories,

And the love that binds us, for eternity.

Liquid Solace

Whiskey rocks

Risky thoughts

Burning herb

Bunch of nerds

Sipping slow

Lost in flow

Pune streets

Echoing beats

But here within

There's naught to win

Or lose or gain

Just souls in pain

Seeking solace

In liquid grace

Listening stories

Sharing memories

Longing come

Like a drum

Beating loud

In the crowd

But tonight

It feels right

To be here

Without fear

Let the past

Fade at last

In dim lit room

In hours of gloom

Let the music play

As we sway,

As the night gives way,

To a new day,

And a new way.

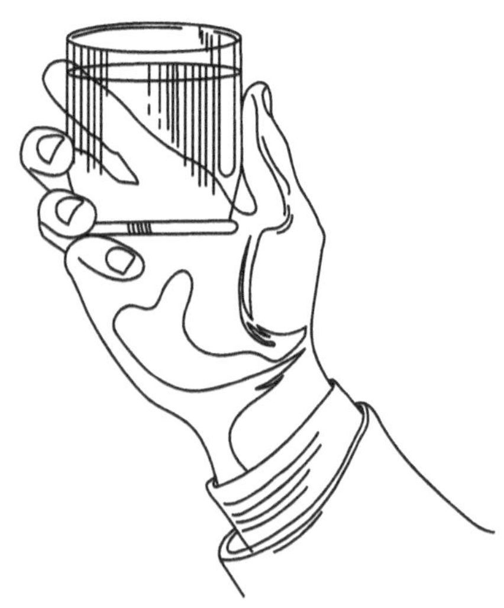

Masking My Emotions

Here I am again,

Hiding love, suppressing pain,

Out of wits, trying be stay sane,

Unproductive without a gain.

It shouldn't have to be like this here,

This cold heart still cares,

In a hush-hush without tears,

Even if alone like an isolated mare.

Farewell

I sit by the shore
Just like we used to do
Watching ripples of memories
of when our love was true

Amidst the rustling leaves, I hear
your words, soft and clear,
Whispering on the breeze,
A song only for us, my dear.

I close my eyes, focus on your face,
For one last time, I whisper goodbye,
And drift into the quiet space,
Where love lingers, and hearts never die.

One Night Stand

I told myself I moved on,
but who was I kidding?
Told myself I was fine,
but the mind's a damn liar,
a broken record.

So I tried one of those dating apps,
Told myself it'd help me forget,
maybe give me the illusion of closure.
And prove to the world I wasn't a guy who'd rot alone
on the shelf.

It's a match!
My phone beeped,
This happened for a few times,
My confidence boosted twice,
Maybe thrice,
And there was this one match catching my eye,
She looked exactly like you.

Who knew what was about to happen
within a minute texting with her!?

She was not there for chocolate and flower,
A rare incident I encountered first hand,
A girl asking for a one night stand.

We met that night.
The wind carried a chill as I waited outside the bar,
my heart drumming louder than my footsteps.
She appeared, bathed in the city's glow,
a shadow of someone I used to know.
She greeted me with a smile, but it wasn't like yours—
not the kind that travels to the eyes.
Her perfume hung heavy in the air,
sharp and sweet, but it wasn't your scent—
that faint trace of lavender you always wore.

Her cherry-pink lips moved toward mine,
soft as silk, cold as truth.
We kissed, and kept on kissing,
but when tongues collided, that spark was missing.
In a cheap motel room,
we undressed under flickering light,
two strangers draped in shadows.
Her nails clawed at my back,
leaving shallow trails, but my skin was numb to it all.

Eyes met when we were undressing each other,
She looked into my eyes, but hers searched for
someone else altogether.

We moved on the sheets, her breath fast, pleading,
"Harder," she gasped.
So I did.
Maybe she thought bruises could erase his fingerprints,
hickeys could smother the sound of his voice.
But her body trembled,
and it wasn't from pleasure.
For the first time, I felt like I was fucking,
Just making more toes curl,
Not making love.

My hands on her hips felt foreign,
like I was gripping sand slipping through my fingers.
Her nails dug into my back, but not to pull me closer—
just to hold on to something, anything.

And me?
I kissed her neck, tasted salt on her skin,
her sweat mixing with mine, and still, it was you—
your laugh, your sighs,
your lip caught between your teeth— haunting me.

I tried to lose myself in her moans,
in the heat of her skin against mine, but instead,
I found you— in the spaces between.

When it was over, she curled away from me,
a silence louder than my thoughts.
Her body there, her mind elsewhere.
I wanted to ask, "Do you see him too?"
But I already knew the answer.

She left before sunrise,
her scent lingering on my sheets,
her warmth fading from my pillow.
And me? I lay there, staring at the ceiling,
the weight of the night crushing my chest.
Because while my body was with her,
I spent the night with you.

Fifth Stage

As I sit upon the shore, waves gently caressing my feet,
The sunset paints the sky with hues of gold and crimson heat.
But within my heart, a sorrow deep and true,
For I mourn the loss of a future shared with you.

Denial, like the tide that ebbs and flows, engulfs my mind,
I yearn to believe that our love won't be left behind.
The ocean whispers soothingly, denying the truth so clear,
But deep down, I know our paths diverge, and I tremble with fear.

Anger crashes against the rocks, fierce and unrestrained,
Like the raging sea, my emotions surge, untamed.
I hurl my frustration at the heavens, demanding answers why,
Why must our love be a casualty, as the sun bids goodbye?

Bargaining, a gentle plea whispered to the fading light,
I beseech the fading sun to grant me one more night.

Depression settles upon the shore, a heavy shroud of gray,
Like the fog that veils the distant horizon, my joy fades away.
I walk along the desolate beach, tears mixing with the sand,
For the future I had dreamed with you slips through my trembling hands.

Acceptance dawns as the last rays of sunlight gently fade,
I watch as the stars emerge, a celestial serenade.
Though grief still lingers within my heart, I find solace in the night,
For in the vast expanse of the universe, new dreams take flight.

So as I sit upon the shore, watching the sunset's final embrace,
I release my pain, surrendering to the beauty and its grace.
Though you won't be part of my future, I let go with a sigh,
For the ocean's vastness reminds me that life goes on, and so shall I.

Possibility

Love Filling

I sit in the dental chair,

Eyes half closed, mouth open wide,

As she probes and pokes and cleans

And I can't help but feel inside

A warmth, a flutter, a rush of blood

As I gaze up at her face,

Her eyes so clear, her smile so bright

My heart begins to race.

I try to focus on the ceiling

And the patterns of the tile,

But my mind keeps drifting back

To the sound of her voice and her smile.

The way she leans in close to me

To check my teeth and gums,

The scent of minty toothpaste

Mixed with her perfume, it numbs.

And, I dare not speak a word

For fear of breaking this illusion,

And so I simply lie here, absurd

Lost in the depths of my confusion.

These thoughts and feelings that I have
For my dear dentist, so kind,
For fear of awkwardness and rejection
And a fractured state of mind.

I don't know what to do or say,
this crush has me in a bind,
but I know I'll be back again someday,
hoping to see her smile, one of the kind.

For in this moment, time stands still
And all that matters is her touch,
And though my heart may ache and thrill
I know, in the end, it's not much.

So as I lie here, in the chair
With her touch upon my lips,
I'll simply close my eyes, aware
That love is but a fleeting eclipse.

Transfixed

The girl in black, she was alone
Beneath the blazing sun's hot glare
Her eyes shut tight, her face tilted
A jhumaka glinting in her hair

Her skin, the color of caramel
Soft and smooth like silk
Her hair, a cascade of midnight
Framing her face like a work of art

I cannot help but stare
Lost in the moment, lost in her
The sun seems to worship her
Bathing her in a golden glow

Her eyes remain closed, lost in thought
Perhaps dreaming of far-off lands
Or lost in the rhythm of her own heart
I do not know, but I am captivated

I watch her, transfixed, as if in a dream,
A vision so ethereal, a mesmerizing scene,
My soul feels a pull, a yearning so strong,
A desire to be near her, to belong.

Her beauty is a mystery,
A puzzle waiting to be solved,
The secrets of her soul hidden deep,
Her heart a fortress, untold.

I long to know her, to unravel her tale,
To dive deep into her mind and soul,
To understand the mystery, to unlock the key,
To be the one to make her whole.

But for now, I'll stand and watch in awe,
As she stands there, lost in reverie,
A beautiful girl in black Indian attire,
With a jhumaka swaying in the breeze.

Tainted

I am the dramatic romantic,
Who keeps you always out of reach,
For I am married to the darkness,
And cleanse myself in bleach.

My skin, already scarred and tainted,
By the scars of pain and strife,
I hide away, afraid to be touched,
Living a solitary life.

I am not made for love, it seems,
But still, I savor every kiss,
And gladly drown in the sweetness,
Of moments such as this.

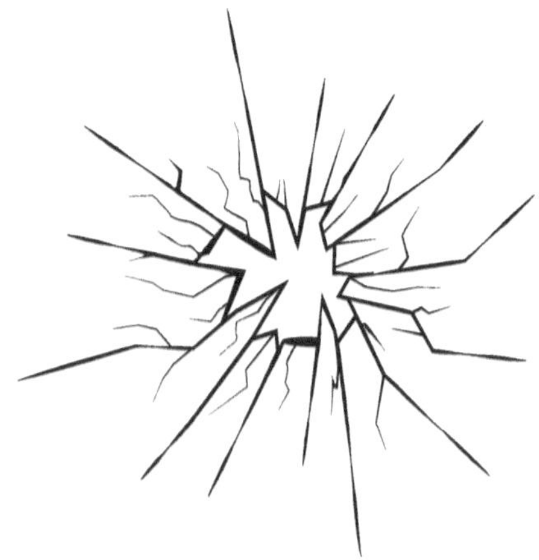

Mamihlapinatapai

As I waited at the traffic signal, amidst the ceaseless
roar of the city,
The scent of the bustling streets, and the distant sound
of a horn -
All of these sensory details stirred something deep
within me.

And then, my eyes fell upon a figure, selcouth and
enigmatic.
A living embodiment of everything that was beautiful in
the world.

And then, my eyes met hers.
In that moment, time stood still,
And I was lost in the enchanting mamihlapinatapai that
we shared.

Her beauty, like a rare gem,
Shone brightly in the midst of the chaos around us.

The green light beckoned,
And she disappeared into the throng of people,
Leaving me with a clandestine that I couldn't shake.

And though she was gone in an instant,

The memory of her lingered on.

I could still hear the sound of her footsteps,

See the way her hair danced in the breeze,

And feel the warmth of her gaze upon me.

The girl at the traffic signal had awakened something

within me,

Something that had been long dormant.

But in that brief moment, something had shifted,

And I knew that I would never be the same again.

And for that, I will always cherish her,

And the moment we shared,

As a reminder of the beauty that exists in the everyday.

Poetry

Modern Literature

I'm rarest of the rare

More like a solar super flare

Leave it you can't comprehend

I'm blessed with something godsend

With the talent of making words rhyme,

Capable of teleporting readers every goddamn time,

To places in their memory or their fantasy,

Sometimes they cry, sometimes there's ecstasy.

You will say

there are others too,

Who got the same old cliche

To offer to you.

Authenticity has gone scanty,

Copy of a copy of a copy is becoming trendy.

As a millennial and as a poet,

Can't stand people calling posers so lit.

Your falling attention span,

Is depriving you,

From what real connection can,

But even several flings can't do.

World is conceiving wrong notion of poetry,
And even we're guilty,
For ignoring them just as different,
Labeling fart as a scent.

All they want is your attention to fuel their number,
Turning a single sentence to poetry by pressing enter.
Whereas we cater verses with subliminal thought in it.
Same words give deeper meaning every time you
revisit.

Social Media

Social media, a world,
full of people seeking validation,
Acedia, a word,
Sinful in chapel, feeling of alienation.

Slave to the numbers,
Bystanders to the new norm.
Crave for more followers,
Influencers go perform.
Give quantity to fetch more supporters,
Butchers of their own artform.
Hiding imperfections behind filters,
Faking connections with strangers.
Creating fake personas,
Projecting spark as supernovas.

Consuming content feed by algorithm,
Thousands of likes on shitty posts, while,
Astonishing sonnet read by only a some,
Versatile,
Real talent roaming like ghosts. Invisible.

Undecipherable

If someone meets me,
They will find me calm,
But there are storms of emotions they can't see,
they can't even hear this atheist chanting psalm.

There is a silent war without swords
but guns loaded with shards
of a heart that is now obsolete
Forgotten how to beat.

But I'm good at hiding,
keeping things perfectly encrypt.
Though I share everything and nothing through my
writing,
It is still harder to understand than the Voynich
manuscript.

Doubt & Ego

In the depths of my being, I find myself -
Questioning the authenticity of my craft,
For though I am blessed with a poetic flair,
My verses cut deeper than a surgeon's knife,
But sometimes I wonder, is it all in vain?
Does my work resonate, or get lost without gain?
Am I really as good as they say?
Or is it all just hype, will my skills decay?
Is it all just a facade, a mask that I wear?
 A fragile ego that's constantly in repair?
Am I truly a Maestro, or just playing it hard?
The imposter syndrome tears me apart, hitting me
hard.

The rhymes that flow from my pen are but whispers on
the wind, fleeting and insubstantial.
And yet, I cannot help but feel the pull of the poetic
muse,
the desire to create, to express, to connect, channeling
my potential.

My verse is the voice of a thousand tales,
my rhythm is a beat that never fails.

I sit and write these lines like I'm the best in the biz
But then reality hits me, it simply isn't how I think it is,
I compare myself to the greats, the ones with the skills
Inspiring me to use my quill to spit facts, to heal,
Not just to pay the bills.

They also remind me that, I've got my own voice,
A unique flow that sets me apart, and I've got my own
choice.
My mind is a battleground, my ego the enemy,
Will my words be forgotten or craft my legacy?
I'm battling myself, my own worst critic,
Trying to stay true, while the world tries to mimic.

But I'll keep on writing, giving words to what I'm
thinking,
Honing my craft, writing stories, to show the world what
I can bring.
Doubt and ego may keep taking turns to cloud my
vision,
But I won't deter, as I know the pursuit of poetic truth is
a worthy one.

Cursed

The curse clings to me like a shroud,
Like Karna, robbed of his power so proud,
I am lost in a battle that never ends,
Condemned to suffer, with no amends.

As a writer and a poet, I wield words with care,
But sometimes they betray me, too sharp to bear,
Like a thorn they prick and wound,
A curse that seems to follow me around.

I am Sisyphus, pushing the boulder uphill with all my might,
Only to see it roll back down, a cruel and bitter sight,
Each time I draw closer to goals set for life,
I get trapped in a cycle of struggle and strife.

I long for the happiness and love I seek,
But somehow it remains forever out of reach,
A fate that I cannot shake,
Something I must endure and take.

I cling to hope, like a sailor lost at sea,

Believing that one day I'll find shore, become free,

Riding every tide of hurdles life throws at me, with all my might,

For I'm certain that my future is bright.

Professionalism

New Colleagues

After surviving a concentration camp,

Joy appeared as if I have rubbed the lamp,

Faces emerged that I longed to see,

Shining their lights, shining their lights on me,

First time in person and not just in the G-suite,

I want to say, one more time, to quell the dispute,

Pineapple DOES NOT belong on pizza.

Austin does not belong on the menu, nor does the

Mona Lisa.

Differences aside, we are an assemblage of creatives,

Capable of creating something original and distinctive,

Like movies of Satyajit Ray,

Or the DC/Marvel debate, something that'll stay.

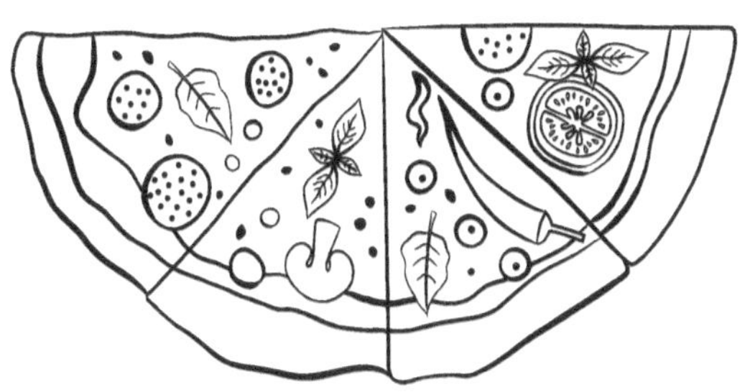

Dawn

In this silence before dawn-
the chaotic circle of the city been complete.
I stop, smile and then move on-
down that empty street.
And I wander on with newfound peace,
As the world awakens slowly, with ease.

Office

In the heart of the city, bustling and bright,

Stands a building of steel, with windows of light

Within its walls, a hub of creative minds,

everyday struggles, everyone grinds.

There sits a team of sharp, witty bards,

Crafting messages that hit their marks.

With pens poised and laptops aglow,

They brainstorm ideas that ebb and flow,

Concepts flying, one after another,

Bringing brands to life, like no other.

Aroma of fresh coffee, brewing strong,

Quick meetings, as always gone too long,

Charts and graphs, lining up the walls,

Concepts taking shape, in conference calls.

Seeking to unlock, the secrets of the crowd,

Insights and data, speaking clear and loud.

Jingles, taglines, clever copy in sight,

All designed to capture the public's delight.

Whiteboards filled with plans, ideas and strategies,
Post-its scattered across desks, lists of endless
priorities.
Designers at their desks, creating logos and visuals with
flair,
Copywriters with their laptops, crafting headlines with
care,
Analytics gurus crunching numbers to measure success,
Social media mavens crafting posts to impress.
Measuring ROIs, and gauging success,
They all aim high and reach nothing less.
Collaboration and creativity, in every nook and cranny,
Spirited debates and moments of levity aplenty.

From concept to final pitch,
This is where advertising and marketing magic enrich,
A place where creativity and business collide,
And nurtures brands worldwide.

False Consciousness

What if I tell you, you are nothing but a cash cow?
A corporate slave, chasing the money,
The system steals all that wealth you gain,
By creating a delusional reality,
Spreading lies carved deep in your brain.
Look around, what do you see?
Do you really think you're free?
Wars, poverty, debts and sea levels all rising side by side.
And the wealth gap is gaping wide.
This is happening in front of you,
You know it too well,
But, you're fallen into a common madness,
That money is the only path to joy,
That beauty is an hourglass shape and fair skin,
So you buy products, join gyms,
because healthy means thin.

Oh, wait, who cares?
We love this game of power and cash,
A game ruled by a handful few,
But friend, you can't really bite off more than what you can chew.

Always comparing, competing,
Chasing bigger homes, bigger cars,
Feeding conflicts, Crying for wars.
They divide and conquer,
And you?
You buy and sell and work and buy again!
End of this greed is nowhere in sight,
All you get is alienation, depression and mental pain.

They win every time,
Keep the oppressed oppressed
And prevail powerful in play.
Lying to you in a glorious way.

So fall back in line,
With forgotten dreams,
Obey their commands,
Your labor spent,
Filling their pockets,
While yours stay empty.

You see all these,
Don't you, honey?
But you prefer that sweet illusion;
Life, liberty and the pursuit of Money.

Pensive

Me & Cosmos

I'm but a speck of dust.
An imperfect child of the universe.
Gliding with the wind,
But in my mind,
I'm on my adventure,
To someplace unseen;
To some state attainable.

In this journey,
Life unfolds an irony,
When I sit here in solitude,
Reciting that I don't care,
As I scroll through old memories.
Wondering will I ever be over this. And when.

There's something
In this loneliness,
Those quiet moments,
They hold you. That's all they do.
Until the fears subside. Until the tears dry.
And you start to believe
That at that moment
Nothing can hurt you.

There I have found a solution,
Maybe all I need is to shed some load.
The lighter the faster.
Dumping baggage,
To be a step closer.
But if I could,
I would have already.
Already living a life I didn't plan.
A tragedy.
It's impossible to explain,
But I'll get over everything,
In just a few years.
I'll survive every whirlwind of emotions,
I'll cross every river of fears.

Some might say I changed.
But now there's no turning back.
No more white flags,
When my self-respect is under attack.

In pleasing others,
And following by their orders,
I made myself a failure.
And that's blame on me not them.
It's my ship and I'm the sailor.

Hope

In the corners of my mind, a maelstrom brews,
Thoughts careening through, twisted and confused.
A never-ending echo, a distorted cry,
Rages on relentlessly, refusing to die.

The fury builds, unbridled and intense,
Pulverizing dreams, leaving no defense.
Gasping for air, amidst the pouring rain,
I struggle to escape this never-ending pain.

And yet, even amidst the stormy strife,
There glimmers a hope that lights up life.
A tiny spark, that struggles to shine,
Amidst the turmoil and chaos of my mind.

It's the hope that tells me I am not alone,
That there are others who feel as I do, unknown.
That there is a way out of this murky haze,
That I can find the light, and escape this maze.

So I cling to this hope, with all my might,

For it's the only thing that keeps me upright.

Through the raging winds and pounding rain,

I know that the hope will help me sustain.

Memory of Days Gone By

The kite, ensnared and motionless,
Caught in the jacaranda tree's grip,
Amidst the spring's vibrant blossom,
Frozen at this moment, time's slip.

Beneath, a non-functioning fountain,
A rusted testament to days gone by,
Its silence speaks of memories once certain,
Now lost to the ebb and flow of time's tide.

Here, a stillness lingers in the air,
As the kite and tree hold their embrace,
A snapshot of beauty and despair,
A moment captured in nature's grace.

Ideal

I'm fighting myself,

To win a few points in this game called life.

Yet somehow I'm always lost.

I'm picking myself up,

To get back from where I fall,

V shape body, well groomed, master of persuasion.

Gentleman in everyone's consideration.

But it's tough,

And things are getting more rough.

I've now seen glimpses of my intrepid form,

For whom carpe diem is the new norm.

No endless bucket list,

No FOMO,

No constant noise buzzing in my head.

There is now my purpose in which I tread.

Concealed emotions

Would you care to hear my tale?
The one that's true and real?
Perhaps you shouldn't seek it in the endless streams of
text,
that flood my phone's bright screen,
nor in my list of calls.

The genuine emotions,
they only surface
when I grasp my pen,
And spill my heart upon the page,
Composing a letter to a friend,
Describing my situation in helpless rage.
The latter that I never send.

That story has been lost
somewhere in words that never escaped my lips,
Even if I share it with another,
it's a weakened rendition at best.
Because I have freed myself
from the intensity of that feeling,
I have to bleed that on that paper,
It will remain forever hidden in that unsent letter.

Silence

My lips once unsettled,
Forming words and emitting sounds,
Now quite quiet.

For some, I have faded
With fading talks.
While some longs,
To hear me ramble,
Which once was annoying to them.

Now that I've distanced myself,
From everything and everyone,
I am walking back to my real self.
Now that I've embraced the silence,
I am hearing myself more.

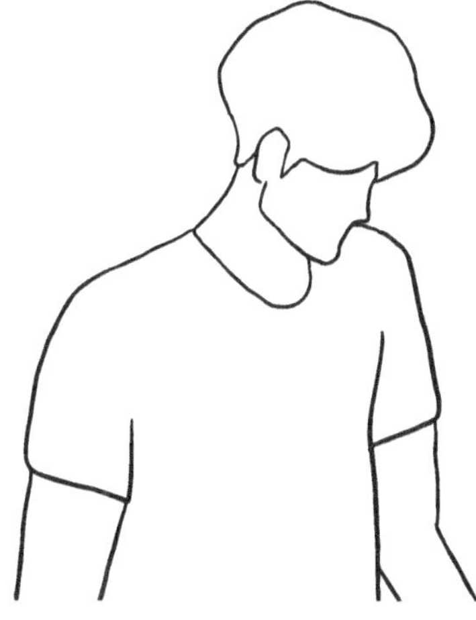

Cool

Growing old, and what it means to be cool,
A shifting tide, a changing rule,
Once it was leather jackets and slicked back hair,
Now it's branded sneakers and baggy wear.

The music we listened to, the shows we watched,
Are now classics, outdated, not hip, but botched,
Our idols have aged, their faces lined with time,
And the youth of today, they see us as past prime.

We used to rebel, against the norm, against the system,
But now we pay taxes and conform, is that wisdom?
We traded our dreams for a steady paycheck,
Is that being cool, or is that just a lack of neck?

Our tastes have evolved, our bodies have slowed,
We're no longer young, we're no longer 'cool', I have
been told.
Even I no longer try fitting in with the crowd,
But standing out, and being proud.

So let's embrace our wrinkles, our graying hair,
And all the knowledge we've gained through the years,
For being cool is about being true to who we are,
And living life to the fullest, no matter how far.

Growing old doesn't mean we lose our edge,
It just means we've learned to embrace life's pledge,
And while the definition of cool may change with time,
We'll always be cool, in our own unique rhyme.

Guilt

Crying, alone in a dark room,

With pathetic thoughts flowing through my mind,

Questioning my existence,

For having you trapped in a nasty situation,

The mayhem I created,

For starting domino that led to everything you said,

Every action you've taken,

Every breath of mine seems like a sin,

For the crime I committed.

Fake Friend

In the depths of my sorrow,

I am but a mere shadow,

Haunted by the ghosts of my past,

A prisoner of my own remorse at last.

I'm a fake friend, not true at all,

I didn't respect, didn't hear your call,

I called myself your confidante,

But I didn't deserve that title to flaunt.

My heart is heavy with regret,

For I have caused you so much upset,

I wish I could undo what I've done,

And mend what I have broken, one by one.

Alas, time moves forward with haste,

Leaving me to confront my own disgrace,

I am but a lost soul, wandering aimlessly,

In search of redemption, and a way to be free.

Oh, how I wish to make things right,

And to lift the darkness that clouds my sight,

But for now, I must accept my fate,

And wait patiently for a chance to escape.

For even in the depths of despair,

I hold on to a glimmer of hope, so rare,

That someday, somehow, I might find a way,

To make amends, and finally have my say.

Simulation

As I peer into the mirror's embrace,

My thoughts drift into a nebulous space.

Does this reflection reveal who I am,

Or just a facade, a mirage, a sham?

The chill of glass runs under my finger,

Drawing me in, my thoughts now linger.

Black and white, in sharp juxtaposition,

The mirror reveals the depths of my intuition.

Am I a mere puppet in a complex simulation,

Confined to the limits of a digital creation?

Glitches and uncertainties gnaw at my core,

Forcing me to question what I thought I knew before.

The Roads Taken

A child takes his first steps, into a world unknown,

His heart heavy with dreams, and fears overblown.

He knows not of the many paths

Of life's twists and turns, and its aftermaths.

The roads ahead, they all seem bright

And he walked with a skip in his stride

But as time ticked by, and years go past

His feet grew weary, his pace didn't last

Now he looks back at the roads he has trod

The ones he skipped, the ones that clawed

At his heart and soul, right or wrong,

the people he has met, the ones he has lost,

Contributing a verse to his life's song.

He remembers the joy, the love,

the moments of pure bliss,

the laughter, the smiles,

and the passion, the sweet kiss.

But then the memories turn sour,
and his heart begins to ache,
as he recalls the pain, the hurt,
the mistakes he couldn't shake.

He wishes he could turn back time,
and undo the choices he has made,
erase the scars, heal the wounds,
and strengthen relations that have faded.

He wonders how he has come this far
He wonders if he has lost his way,
If the journey was worth the price he had to pay.

He thinks of all the unexplored paths
That he never dared to try
And all the ones that led to pain
That he wished he could deny

His end looms ahead
He's out of choices, the roads are dead
And now he sees, with crystal clear sight
The roads he chose weren't quite right.

For every left and every right
He made a choice, in the heat of the fight
And now he knows, it's all too late
The roads he chose have sealed his fate.

Belief

Oh, religion, the tapestry of faith
A woven cloth of every hue and wraith
You are the prayer and the meditation
You are solace in times of devastation

Opium of the masses
A drug to dull the pain
A false hope for the hopeless
A tool for the rich to maintain

A profound, psychological response
An internal, eternal renaissance
Contemplating unknown, the mystery that we confront
In our outer world and inner selves,
A yearning for meaning that constantly delves
Into the riddles of life and death
The questions that echo with every breath

This spiritual need, as real as hunger
The fear of death that makes us ponder
We seek connection and a sense of place
And a way to transcend time and space

But I can't overlook the warning signs
Of how you've been used to draw dividing lines
To justify hate and maintain power
Exploiting the vulnerable hour after hour.

Rain Is Not For Everyone

In the rhythm of the pouring rain,
Whispers secrets, not all can attain,
For rain is not for everyone, my dear,
It's a gift, a message, perfectly clear.

It kisses the earth with cleansing grace,
A tender touch on each upturned face,
But not all hearts can feel its song,
In the rain's embrace, where dreams belong.

Some seek shelter from the stormy night,
Afraid to dance in the moon's soft light,
For rain is not for everyone, they say,
Yet in its tears, souls find their way.

It waters the roots of ancient trees,
Nurturing life with effortless ease,
But not all eyes can see its art,
The rain's symphony that fills the heart.
To those who cherish the drops that fall,
They hear the stories, they heed the call,
For rain is not for everyone, it's true,
But for those who listen, it whispers through.

Protest

Dirty Politics

Like goats being led to slaughter,
By the very people who raised her.
Politicians keep butchering their ideology,
Justifying everything by teleology.

Horsetrading is just a part of the game,
Pandits, media houses 'praise' the same.
Dirty politics is no more a surprise,
they do it all right before our eyes.

And what do we do?
Label them as modern-day Chanakya,
Give their cunningness respect,
If that's our reaction,
Why will they ever stand up for what's morally correct?

Government is government, we must make a fuss,
for We Are The People,
and as The People, we must!
It's always a lose-lose for us.
We choose a lesser evil,
But he ends up joining hands with worse.
Our silence, for our country, is the worst curse.

revoCABable moNaRCh

They have the number,

They have the majority,

Time to wake up from slumber,

Time to wreak up their bigotry.

Stopping 'em from repeating historic blunder.

Stopping from burning the nation's identity to fuel their politics.

Our silence is assumed to be an ideological surrender.

Let dissent be exhumed to fight these hypocrites.

Why only those three countries?

Why not all neighborhood religious minorities?

If you say 'they' have 54 other choices to choose a new country,

Isn't that in line with Jinnha's two-nation-theory?

India was always secular,

It didn't become one in 1947,

Never discriminated any religion,

India ever demonstrated peace. Our heaven.

They want a Pakistan's clone, a Hindu Rashtra,

So-called patriots are tearing down national legacy.

But we are the followers of the great secular king of Maharashtra,

Maharaj, Chhatrapati Shivaji.

Sick Society

A frenzied mind, a rapid pace,
A thousand lies we can't erase,
Deceptive headlines and twisted views,
How can we tell what is true news?

The sickness spreads like wildfire,
Mass disease, we can't retire,
Fake smiles and happy faces,
Masks hiding darker places.

Pesticides in our food,
Nature's goodness is subdued,
Another dead field, barren land,
No longer can we make a stand.

Icebergs melting, oceans rise,
Deserts forming before our eyes,
Maniacs leading nations,
The world's on fire, no salvation.

Woke

While calling myself a Bhagat Singh fan,
I support the demolishing of Lenin's statue,
I'm a woke man sharing my political view.

I'm complaining how shitty this lockdown is,
Though I've all the luxuries,
I'm still mad at these inconvenient working conditions,
But I'm raising questions at Savarkar's mercy petitions.

Legends who fought against casteism,
Shahu, Phule, Ambedkar,
Am I making them biggest iconoclasts victim of asteism,
When I call them as leaders of my caste?
Casting vote to a person of the caste I'm associated to,
I'm a woke man sharing my political view.

Let alone knowing what Marxism is all about,
I haven't even truly understood what's left and right.
But since my leader is calling them wrong,
I chorus the same hatred song.

Here's something I won't ever tell,

I really don't know history that well,

But I'm learning through WhatsApp University,

And spreading the same info with all my capacity.

Even at a time when I think my leader was wrong,

I stay with my herd, clapping along.

The self-proclaimed spokesman in me defends him,

Wherever I go, self-proclaimed spokesman in me, toil there,

If not in my relationship, at least I'm loyal here.

War

Detonators blowing
Every now and then
Causing tender ears of kids to bleed
Mines are placed,
Roads blocked
People being checked.
Harassed and stripped.

Feeble cries
Lost in the roar of the deafening blasts.
Roads soaked in blood.
But you're busy greasing your muscles.
Celebrating your "victory"
Naming your massacre a defeat of the enemy.

Killing thousands in the name of nation or religion.
To claim it is more peaceful!?
Both mere concepts.
manmade.
Now killing men.

The human race has gone mad.

Earth becoming a living hell.

In name of peace, people are being chopped into pieces.

For the love of religion, hatred is being perpetuated

In name of the nation, innocent soldiers are being killed.

When the real troublemakers stay away from the war zone.

Living a life of luxury.

Poors pay for their deeds,

Die fighting their war.

Monochromatic Patriotism

Carrying the divine glory,
Legacy of the greatest of the great,
An epic story,
With a billion characters,
Shaping Vishwaguru's fate.

There lay the legendary artists, saints, and kings,
On this soil of Hindustan
It's time for our generation to expand our wings,
Fly to new heights, creating a new history,
Our new dastaan.

But let's spend some time to know what it means to be
an Indian first,
Understand the spirit of a nation's core,
Not just slicing through an apparent crust.

Since ancient time,
When ethnic cleansing was a service to immortal,
And not a crime,
So was the prosecuting religious minority,
But, India was the land of harmonious heterogeneous
diversity.

I often wonder,
How India's patriotism can become so monochromatic?
Black and white,
One comment, one opinion,
And boom… you're either a traitor or true patriotic.

Biased and divided,
Eager to label us.
Sickular, libertard, pseudo-intellectual, Anti-national.
For living up to our true cultural values? for following
the Indian ideal?
Zombie minds serving for their leader's political motive,
Spoiling the thousands of years old, my county's grand
narrative.

Don't you think acting against subversive behaviour is
patriotic. And not treasonous?
Isn't asking questions and constructive criticism
productive. And not dangerous?

Let's pledge to become an actively participating citizen,
Use every authority enshrined in the Constitution.
In the era of narrow hypernationalism,
Let's preach universal brotherhood;
An idea advocated by our great nation!

Rise Up

The system built and run by lies,
Should crumble, may masses see beyond crocodile
cries,
Beyond every type of imaginary division,
May all rational rebels work for a greater vision.

Let's not be afraid to speak up, to challenge the norm,
Let us raise our voice, sounding the alarm,
Through the tangled web of division and strife,
Let us forge a path towards a brighter life.

So join me, let's rise up and make a change,
We'll break the chains, break down the cage,
We'll create a world that's true and free,
Rational rebels, that's you and me.

Prism

They say our existence is against the religion,

The world is a prism,

But their thoughts have a different conclusion.

They think the angles are only three,

He, she, and everyone that shouldn't be.

They think in this world queer doesn't belong,

And our being is nothing but wrong.

Their love is love and ours a hideous sight.

What they see is the rainbow we form,

But can't notice that we are essentially the same light.

It's just when we enter the prism of sexuality,

you pass straight, and we create diversity.

Remove that prism, we, like you, are part of humanity,

We are the same light.

Then why is there hate, discrimination and insanity?

Why are we still fighting this fight?

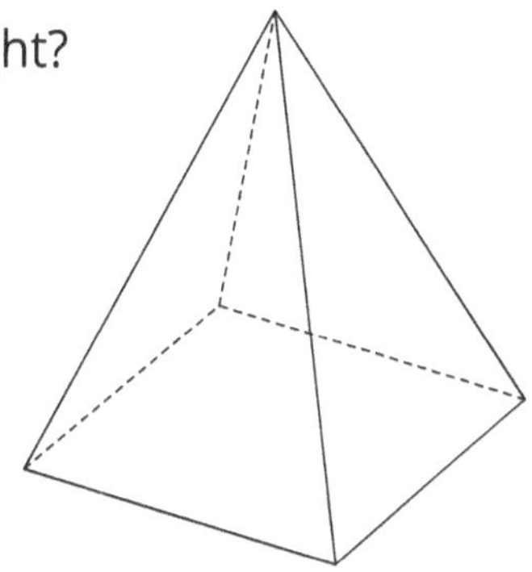

Partake

Injust Silence

When injustice seeps like poison into our veins,
And apathy, a moral decay, perpetuates its reign,
The world shudders in dissonance, a deafening roar,
And the cries of the oppressed, louder than ever before.
Their pain trembles the earth's very core,
And their hopelessness falls like an endless downpour.

Our silence allows oppressor's hand to thrive,
And tyranny spreads like vines that entwine.
Inaction and fear let oppression grow,
Justice's call remains unheard, a whisper low.

Allies are needed, like the roots of a tree,
Strength and support - a shelter for the free.
We must amplify their voice, loud and clear,
And fight for the right, unyielding, without fear.

History's pages have taught us well,
Protests are needed to quell -
the forces of injustice that loom.
And support the marginalized to bloom.

Our voices, like a tempest's fierce wind,

Shall bring the change we all seek to bind.

For in this struggle, we shall find our unity,

And rise victorious, like a phoenix from its calamity.

Building A Better World

The system built and run by lies,
Should crumble, may masses see beyond crocodile
cries,
Beyond every type of imaginary division,
May all rational rebels work for a greater vision.

Let's not be afraid to speak up, to challenge the norm,
Let us raise our voice, sounding the alarm,
Through the tangled web of division and strife,
Let us forge a path towards a brighter life.

Let us not merely dream, but with purpose we shall act,
With unwavering conviction, and the courage to impact,
Let us tear down the walls of hate,
And build a world that's fair and great.

For we are the hope and the change we seek,
We are the ones who can turn the tide and reach the
peak,
Let us rise up, and let our voices be heard,
For in our unity lies the power to transform the world.

Awakening

A wedding day, a hot and steamy morn
The sun beats down, relentless and warm
A procession winds through city streets
My Brahmin friend, the groom swaying with the beats

But whispers and jeers were all I could hear
As the caste system's weight pressed in, clear
The bride's home is a hive of activity
But I sense a hostility, an unwelcome proclivity

The attendees, they sneer and they snub
My presence at this wedding, they loudly dub
Abuse and insults, they hurl my way
It's all so direct, I don't know what to say
My heart is heavy, my spirit crushed
The manusmriti reigns, it's all so unjust

Tears fall from my eyes as I leave the scene
I can't bear this burden, this weight so obscene
I return home, my father's there
He listens, he understands, he shows he cares.

Thomas Paine's words rang true and clear,
Education was the key, to break free from fear,
To empower the oppressed, the shudras and women,
And fight for their rights, now my life's mission.

And so I set out, my spirit renewed
To build a better world, for the many, not just a few
To spread awareness, to educate and empower
To be a force for change, in every moment and every hour

For education, I believe, is the key
To unlock the doors of opportunity
To break down the walls of caste and class
To create a world, where all can surpass

The road ahead is long, the journey tough
But with each step, my resolve grows enough
For I know in my heart, that change may not come soon,
but I should try,
To fight for justice, until the day I die.

Jallianwala

I am witness to a tragedy
A tale of pain and horror
Of a peaceful gathering
That turned into a slaughter

In Jallianwala Bagh, on that fateful day,
We gathered, seeking justice in our own way,
But as we stood there, quiet and brave,
Demanding the release of our leaders and freedom we
crave.

The bullets rained down upon us like thunders,
As the blood begins to spill,
And the tears of a thousand martyrs,
Flooded the land until it's still.

Blood mixed with gunpowder – that scent –
Was messing my brain, then there was a brutal sound,
As the screams of the innocent,
Echoed across the ground.

Blood mixed with gunpowder – that scent –
Was messing my brain, then there was a brutal sound,
As the screams of the innocent,
Echoed across the ground.

Amidst the chaos, I found myself
Fleeing to a nearby house for safety
But what I found there was even worse
A room filled with death and tragedy.

I spent my night crying and watching
As hundreds of corpses lay around
Their lives cut short in a senseless act
Of violence that knew no bound.

The next day, I emerged from the house
To a scene of unimaginable horror
The park was filled with lifeless bodies
A sight that left me forever altered.

But even amidst the disaster and distress
There were stories of heroism and grace
Of those who sacrificed themselves
To save others from this brutal fate.

The memories of those who fell,
Became a spark for the living,
A call for freedom and justice,
And a new beginning.

So when you remember that day,
Think how freedom came at a great price they had to
pay,
And take a pledge to continue their fight,
For a world where justice and peace can finally take
flight.

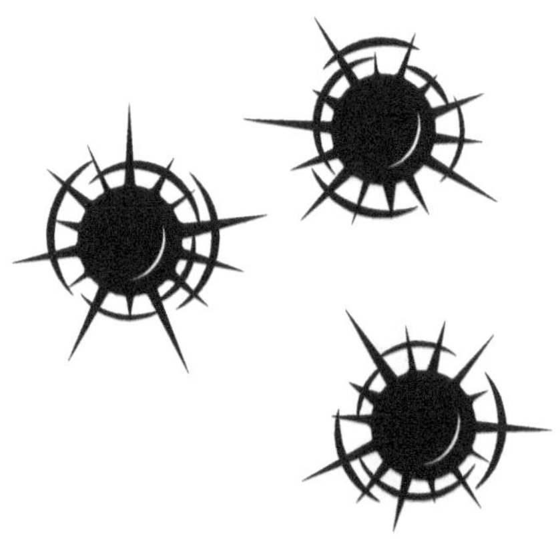

Wake-Up Call

The morning dew still clings to the leaves,
And the world awakens with a gentle ease,
As I lay in bed with my eyes still closed,
A sound fills my ears, and my heart is exposed.

The chirping of birds, so sweet and clear,
Fills me with joy, and I shed a tear,
For in this concrete jungle, they are rare,
Their sweet songs a gift, beyond compare.

As I lay here, listening to their call,
I cannot help but feel so small,
For they are the bio-indicators of our world,
Their decline, a sign of what we have unfurled.
Like tigers in forests, they are a sign,
Of the health of our planet, our design,
And as I lay here, I can't help but see,
How our actions have caused such misery.

But in this moment, I am filled with bliss,
As I listen to their song, a moment of pure happiness,
For in their sweet chirping, I can see,
A world of hope, a future where they are free.

Prevalence

Betrayed By Trust

She was feeling like being Medusa,

Similar story,

Different time,

His sin,

And she was guilty.

As if she was the one who had committed the crime.

The "R-word" was messing with her head,

"He's a nice guy, no one will believe you"

her friend said.

And asked to forget what he did,

Only if that happens to them, god forbid,

They'll understand her situation.

How he has done lasting devastation,

Without a moment's hesitation.

She just sat there staring into space,

Infirm, immobile, a rare case.

That day, she was with someone familiar,

The mask fell off,

When he started touching her

She saw in him the Devil himself,

Felt betrayed by the trust itself.

Bruising her body,

Unwelcome,

Unwanted,

Forcing himself on her,

He didn't stop.

No! She cried.

Multiple times,

Nothing halted him from climbing atop.

He asked her to wait,

Said she'll like it this time,

He keeps penetrating,

As if her words weren't worth a dime.

Her conscious drifted away,

Words ceased to leave her lips,

Lying on the bed,

Hands tied behind the head.

Did she just have sex?

No, she didn't. She experienced Hell.

And this will remain a secret,

An untold tale.

She did the walk of shame home.
Disappointed, Traumatized.
Like Martin Luther returned from Rome.

With so many questions in the head,
No clear answers in sight.
Who do you turn to when you've been abused?
Will she ever be able to trust/love?
or be loved again?
Her adolescent brain confused, wondered,
Who would want you when you've been used?

Those flashbacks started haunting,
Ruining her once peaceful sleep,
The pain getting harder,
She keeps trying to not weep.
Failed attempts became routine.

He oozed out of her self esteem.
Yet she thinks no one will believe her,
And of course, he won't admit.
But what if come back again,
To repeat 'it'.

Real Men

They say real men don't cry—
Growing up, I heard, real men don't ask, they take.
But when I dared to ask why,
Silence was all they could make.

Real men don't... blah blah blah...
The list kept growing long.
Were they raising us right,
Or simply teaching us wrong?

Molding us into emperors,
With a throne of multiple personalities.
Who weep before the mirror confessor,
Because how will a weak man handle responsibilities?
Keep pretending to be okay,
Even when not.
You should at best be angry but never sad,
As it is effeminate. (What an irony)

But strength isn't silence;
It's facing what others evade.
Encourage your brothers to shed those tears—
To let the flood cascade.

Beyond the iceberg's frozen peak,

Lies a heart both raw and grand.

Perhaps it's time we redefine:

This is the real man.

Prostitute of God

In the temple's sacred hush, I stood,
A Devadasi, adorned in silk and gold.
But beneath the finery, a tale untold,
Becoming "prostitute of God," a story to unfold.

Bound by duty, chained by decree,
They offered my body, but my soul stayed free.
Trained in arts, my spirit alive,
Yet thrust into darkness, where hopes would strive.

Once revered, now cast into despair,
A vessel defiled, a victim unaware.
Yet within me, a flickering flame burned,
Hoping blessings of Yellama for everything I served.

They think my worth is skin-deep alone,
But I dance defiance, a rebellion of my own.
Through tear-stained eyes, searching the light,
A glimpse of freedom, for breaking the night.

So hear my plea, O world that turns blind,

To the stories of those left behind.

See beyond the title, the chains that persist,

And know that I am more than the role I'm assigned.

I am a woman, resilient and brave,

A survivor of darkness, eager to pave —

A path of redemption, where love can reside,

And the Devadasi's voice will no longer hide.

The Casual Culture

In the act of sex, your body turns to ice,

No heat of passion, just a mechanical device.

Each movement, routine,

from past encounters or screen,

No connection, just a false sense of being seen.

Orgasms may come, fleeting moments of bliss,

But when they fade, you're left with a sense of abyss.

If you've known true making love,

An act of becoming whole,

You'll be left with hollow feeling, as if you've sold your soul,

For a moment of pleasure, a mere empty goal.

True love, where the body and soul unite,

Has become a mere concept, like stars in city night.

They are there waiting for you to sought,

For what the soul really wants,

cannot be bought or taught.

Psychotic

Thrill & Trauma

The breeze that played with my hair,
Invited a sense of wonder, a dare,
As I rode my bike on that raw road,
My heart's joy began to unfold.

A sense of adventure, I couldn't deny,
As I rode my bike, beneath the open sky,
My soul alive with newfound joy,
My heart leaping like a child's toy.

But fate, with her capricious hand,
Led me to a sharp, unexpected bend,
My heart racing, my mind a blur,
My bike skidded, my hopes did incur.

The pain I felt, the scars that stayed,
A silent reminder of the price I paid,
And though I drove back, with bruises and ache,
It was the weight of fear that made me shake.

And now, whenever I take to the road,

Fear grips my soul with a firm hold,

My heart sunks, my hands tremble,

As memories of that day assemble.

PTSD is a real thing,

A wound that's hard to heal,

But I'll keep on moving forward,

And learn to live with what I feel.

I'll face my fear, and overcome,

One day, I know I will,

I'll ride my bike with confidence,

And feel that rush, that thrill.

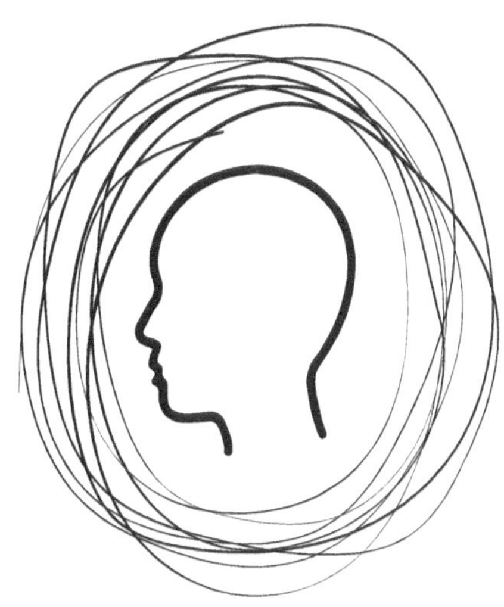

Raising The Dead

It's an auspicious night,

Under full moonlight,

Wearing a diamond-studded crown,

And long silk gown,

Watching candle burning,

Her spirit was yearning,

Time to use the spellbook,

Show her love is not for destiny to took,

She chanted his name,

fired up an eternal flame,

After many sacrifices she has done,

Finally, the main ritual has begun,

Finally capable of casting that special spell,

Bringing him back from hell.

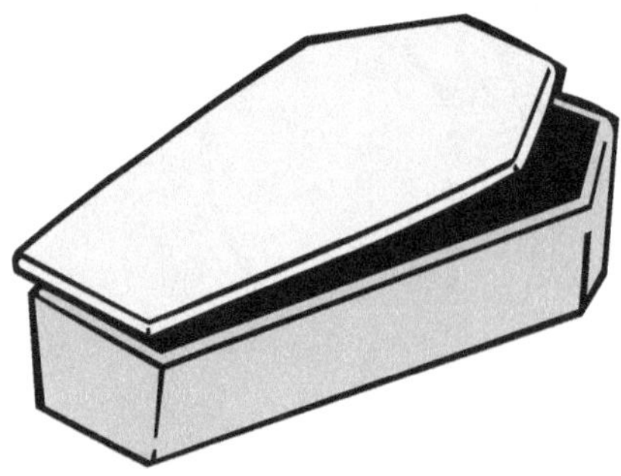

Inner Demons

Sinking into the depths.

Feeling that weight of guilt dragging me again.

Hearing whispers in the darkness,

Sweet lies and the truth that causes pain.

These voices are of the demons inside me.

Demons who holding me tight,

Making me suffocate.

I tried a lot to kill them,

But it seems like they are an integral part of my fate.

They always stay.

Even when everyone else leaves.

Maybe these demons are no one else;

but me.

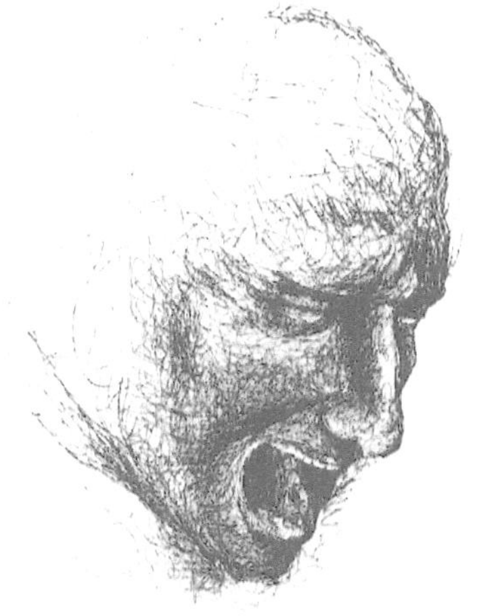

Addicted

As if I'm in the grip of some ancient spell,
Compelled to shop, unable to quell,
The urge to splurge on every tempting find,
Like a siren's call that captures my mind.

Like Pandora, I open shopping app - the box of
temptation,
Knowing full well the consequences that may come,
But unable to resist the allure of material goods,
That promise to fill the void within my heart.

The Amazonian goddesses of commerce and trade,
Smile down upon me as I click and scroll,
Filling my cart with items I do not need,
And charging my card with each impulsive purchase.

The more I buy, the more I crave,
A vicious cycle of desire and consumption,
Like the mythical Tantalus, forever reaching for fruit,
But never quite able to grasp what he longs for.

In the depths of my digital shopping spree,

I am becoming a sort of Jay Gatsby,

Filling my mansion with things to impress and dazzle,

But feeling empty and hollow inside.

I am Icarus, soaring too high too fast,

Fueled by online deals, I thought would last,

But now I am falling, my finances in shambles,

\My addiction to shopping, now an endless gamble.

I yearn for contentment, a life free from greed,

To find peace in the simple things I need,

But for now, I am caught in this cycle of spend,

Until I find a way to break free, and make amends.

Thank you for tolerating me and my strange obsession with rhyming, till the end.

I promise I'll seek help.

Mahesh Mali is an acclaimed Indian poet, bestselling author, and accomplished writer who blends creativity and precision in both art and craft.

Mahesh's writing spans multiple genres, reflecting his deep passion for words and storytelling. However, poetry remains his truest calling. He believes poetry offers unmatched depth and clarity when it comes to expressing the most intimate and universal feelings.

His published works include Reflections of My Youth, Enter, and Meera. Each of these books has resonated with readers for their emotional depth, vivid imagery, and thought-provoking themes.